the smallest part

"Behold, I say unto you, I cannot say

the smallest part

which I feel."

Neal A. Maxwell

Published by Deseret Book Company, Salt Lake City, Utah 1973

Library of Congress Catalog No. 73-87240
ISBN No. 0-87747-505-9

Printed in
U.S.A.
by
Deseret Press

Dedication

To my parents, Clarence and Emma Maxwell: who provided a quiet example, in all seasons, of Christianity in action; who put family and Church first, so that I and my five sisters "did not doubt" our parents knew that the gospel of Jesus Christ is the way and that there is "none other"; who, in their modest circumstances, gave so richly of themselves to their children, and to hundreds of friends and neighbors—

And as well, to two more recently acquired parents, George and Fern Hinckley, who have given me not only steadfast support and encouragement, but who, most of all, prepared so well, and then gave me gladly, that splendid woman, Colleen.

Some Introductory Thoughts

This book's title comes from the poignant words of Ammon (Alma 26:16) as he gloried in God's goodness to mankind—so enthusiastically, in fact, that his brother said, "I fear that thy joy doth carry thee away unto boasting." But Ammon's boasting was of God, and, therefore, his joy was so full that his tongue could not transmit all that Ammon wished he could say: Ammon felt more than he could tell!

So it is with me and this book, for underarticulation pervades these pages.

Ammon was impressed that God would be "mindful of us, wanderers in a strange land"; I am impressed that God is "mindful" of mankind today, an age in which the Christian is "a stranger in the land"—in which Christianity is counterculture in a sea of secularism.

Part I of what follows focuses on strategic matters such as truth, morality, and causality—for how an individual views such things surely determines so much else; different beliefs do produce different behavior! A Christian must be aware, therefore, of the implications of his beliefs, but without making these a condition of his association with his fellowmen.

Part II of the book shifts sharply in style and focuses on tactical, but important, things pertaining to the stewardship of the committed Christian, such as how best to help others, how to manage time, and how to communicate—for our life style and our work are outward expressions of our inner beliefs.

Some graphic illustrations are used precisely because words so often reflect only "the smallest part" of what one wishes to communicate. Quotations from others are also used where these illuminate an idea better than the author can (which is often).

Thus in what follows, there is variety through which the reader can move—but with no guarantees as to its adequacy—only with the assurance that the "table" has been set sincerely.

For friends not familiar with The Church of Jesus Christ of Latter-day Saints, thank you for your patience as you encounter "inside" references, and even occasional jargon—for the welcome to these pages is just as warm for you!

Acknowledgments

No author works alone. He needs, as I did: a venturesome publisher, in this case Wm. James Mortimer; "sources" such as Tony Kimball, who kindly sends me reports back from the intellectual "front lines," and Mildred Keyes, who shares the "finds" in her own reading; a secretary, Laura Castano, who was willing to be patient with my tortured manuscript; "readers" who will care enough to be candid in their reactions to spare other readers at least some pain, as Elizabeth Haglund and Arthur S. Anderson did so diligently with this work; an illustrator willing to set my concepts into a form that enlivens them, as Thomas L. Tyler did in his spare time for me; finally, since life consists of some harsh trade-offs where time is concerned: a family who will not only forgo but who will also encourage the author as did Colleen, Becky and Mike, Nancy and Jane (with Cory urging me on from Central Germany). To all these, and more, my thanks and gratitude, for you have a share in whatever good flows from the pages that follow.

Neal A. Maxwell

Contents

PART ONE

Some Strategic Matters

"If you have not chosen the Kingdom of God, it will make in the end no difference what you have chosen instead."
—William Law, English Clergyman of the 18th Century

1

A View of Truth

"This know also, that in the last days perilous times shall come. For men shall be . . . ever learning, and never able to come to the knowledge of the truth." (2 Timothy 3:1-2, 7.)

"There is no democracy of facts." (Author unknown.)

The Christian's view of truth sets him apart from others in a very strategic way, for there is a profound difference in his valuation of truth—though not necessarily in his fervor for finding out about all kinds of things—and in his view as to what the big issues are.

We live in an age that is flooded with facts and issues, big and small. But, ironically, in some respects men are, as never before, ". . . ever learning, and never able to come to a knowledge of the truth," or of the real issues. The poet, e. e. cummings, described one view of learning when he wrote: "All ignorance toboggans into know and trudges up to ignorance again," a process which would be a reflection of futility as much as humility. Much of the flood flowing from the frontiers of knowledge is very valuable, but in the

deluge of data there are also many insignificant truths. There
are also isolate truths which are, in many respects, like the
isolate individual—both wander in perpetual search of com-
panionship and meaning. Some research is actually undertaken in reaction to the human condition—not to alleviate
it. President John R. Silber of Boston University has observed:

> "One can forget the meaninglessness of his own existence by
> occupying himself with scientific experiments of dubious import.
> Countless scientists and scholars spend their lives in the search of truths
> that are irrelevant to them."

Something can be both true and unimportant. Therefore, just as there are, in Jesus' words, "the weightier matters
of the law," there are "weightier" truths! We must not only
distinguish between fact and fancy, but know which facts
are worthy of fealty.

The gospel of Jesus calls our attention to the reality
that there is an aristocracy among truths; some truths are
simply and everlastingly more significant than others! In
this hierarchy of truths are some which illuminate both history and the future and which give to men a realistic view
of themselves—a view that makes all the difference in the
world.

In this context, one can see how being "learned" (by
simply indiscriminately stockpiling a silo of truths) is not necessarily the same thing as being wise, for wisdom is the dis-
tillation of data—not merely its collection and storage.

So far as is known, the question Pilate put to Jesus,
apparently without expecting the Savior to answer—"What
is truth?"—has been answered only once: the Lord later
said, ". . . truth is knowledge of things as they are, and as
they were, and as they are to come." Truth is a knowledge
of reality—of "things." Some realities are transitory and in-
consequential; some realities maintain themselves everlast-

ingly, or longitudinally, over vast spans of time. In the hierarchy of truth, therefore, some truths describe those realities which persist from age to age—which are more significant than fleeting facts. A knowledge of such central realities as the existence of God and his presiding and purposeful role in the universe, the great rescue mission of his Son Jesus Christ, and of man's co-eternality with our Heavenly Father is sovereign sense! Other gradations of truth reflect knowledge of those things which are often important, but passing and proximate.

In point of value, longitudinal truth, when compared to truth which reflects reality as it exists in only a portion of one of the three great time zones—past, present, and future— is like the Bible when it is compared with the single issue of a newspaper. Telephone directories are useful, but inevitably obsolescent reflections of reality. Many of us still store in our memories old phone numbers, and veterans usually know their military service serial number. These are once useful but now useless facts.

Knowing how, through the process of irrigation, land can be made more productive is actually very useful— proximately—but in terms of ultimate utility, man's need to know about soils does not compare in importance with that knowledge which concerns souls!

Our stunning success in understanding physical nature is well known, but one irony that is little appreciated is the fact that many of the critical data about human nature are already available in the scriptures; these data do not need to be discovered—but merely openly accepted and seriously applied. Cataclysm for the people on this planet is most likely to flow from technology created by men who cannot also tame that technology because they cannot tame themselves by using the taming truths of the gospel of Jesus Christ.

The truth which is most liberating, therefore, involves

a knowledge of the controlling, cosmic realities in the universe. As Paul noted directly (1 Timothy 2:5) "the truth" is: "For there is one God, and one mediator between God and men, the man Christ Jesus." But life and education, of necessity, must be concerned with truths that are related to realities of all kinds—as long as we are not fatally confused about the gradations of truth.

The Savior noted that if we are really serious about our discipleship, and continue in his word, "Ye shall know the truth, and the truth shall make you free." Knowing the truth about those things that really matter frees us from our inhibiting and finite perspective in the same way that turning the light on in an otherwise darkened room can keep us from stubbing toes and breaking furniture.

Plastic freedom, by contrast, is a naive freedom; it is filled with a kind of ersatz exhilaration such as a man might have who is unknowingly speeding along the white rapids of a river that takes him to a Niagara of consequences.

Only the all-pervasive perspectives of the gospel—walking in the bright light of the full truth about man and the universe—can make us free, for to achieve real perspective one must not only, as C. S. Lewis said, "keep the clean sea breeze of the centuries blowing through" his mind, but also those teachings and truths which transcend time.

Thus, while the disciple of Christ is urged by the scriptures to seek out the best books, to learn about history and law and cultures (for Christianity is not a religion of repose —intellectually or behaviorally), he is also given potent reminders that there is no democracy among facts; indeed, there is a harsh, not-to-be-deposed aristocracy among truths, and one must come to final terms with "the truth" cited by Paul—not merely "a short armistice."

Some truth can even be carried forward with us into our resurrected state and will give us "so much the advantage in the world to come," because such truth pertains to those dimensions of physical nature and human nature which will persist. These truths involve a knowledge of things which transcend and cut across all three great time zones. It is the acquisition of these truths which God has stressed through his prophets that should have priority, for they involve a particularized kind of knowledge that most often focuses on things pertaining to human nature and happiness.

When Jesus criticized the lawyers of his time (Luke 11:52), he said they had "taken away the key of knowledge." In the inspired translation of the New Testament, Joseph Smith added five words: "for ye have taken away the key of knowledge, *the fullness of the scriptures.*"

Without the divine disclosures God has given to us, we face all the usual dangers of incomplete information, but these are compounded by cosmic consequences when we are ignorant, or heedless, of these key truths.

We should seek these "key" truths, not simply because such truths are shiningly there, but because it is by their light "that we see everything else!"

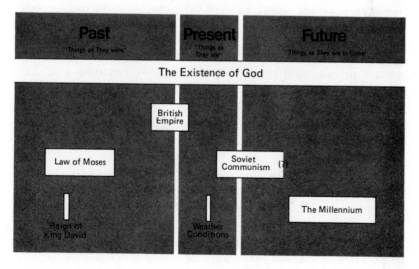

The illustration may help us to understand how some realities, whether these realities are expressed as events or as laws of human nature, persist through all three time zones, but also, though important at the time, how other realities are but a micro-dot on the landscape of history. Therefore, all truth, as a knowledge of various realities, is similar in that respect, but there are inevitable gradations, both in the significance of truths and in our grasp of their implications.

Thus, like the time-lapse photography we see on TV weather shows, clouds come and go, drop their water, shade us, cool us, vex us—but the land and water masses that persist beneath the passing clouds are like the unchanging truths by which men must manage their lives.

This unique approach to truth, far from denigrating reason, gives us added reasons to develop our intellectual powers because, as John Locke said:

"Reason is natural revelation, whereby the eternal father of light, and fountain of all knowledge, communicates to mankind that portion of truth which he has laid within the reach of their natural faculties: revelation is natural reason enlarged by a new set of discoveries communicated by God. . . ."

Hence, to huddle in contentment without extending oneself intellectually and socially merely because one has knowledge of key truths is a betrayal of our trust. When one fails to stretch his "natural faculties," or to use the light God gives him, his is a stewardship gone sour. Brigham Young said:

"The laws that the Lord has given are not fully perfect because the people could not receive them in their perfect fullness; but they can receive a little here and a little there. . . .

"Hence, if you wish to act upon the fullness of the knowledge that the Lord designs to reveal, little by little, to the inhabitants of the earth, we must improve upon every little as it is revealed."

It is no accident that men like Abraham, Moses, and Joseph Smith, who learned to see so much with their "eye of faith," were given splendid supplemental insights about the universe. But God's desire to share must be met by our readiness to receive. We must be appreciative of, and skilled enough to deal with, the truth that is already "within reach" of our natural faculties. By discovering truth in its many independent spheres, and yet still being humble enough to be enlarged by "a new set of discoveries," truth begets truth. Without divine guidance, our cerebral calisthenics, though often fascinating to engage in, can be empty exercise.

Such an approach to knowledge is not other-worldly at all. The key, longitudinal truths are highly relevant because they are irretrievably connected with the very things that matter most "here and now." We need to see more clearly how such cosmic concepts have their mortal implications and consequences. Otherwise, we are apt to be confused about causality—like the weary soldier in the ballad of my old infantry division of World War II, who wanted to avoid any more beachheads: "I don't mind guns, but I can't stand bullets. Don't send me in."

Knowing the truth about "who" man really is involves both his identity and destiny, and the implications of such persistent realities include crucial information about what man's mortal environment should contain for his well being. The institution of the family is at "peril-point," for instance. Professor Urie Bronfenbrenner warns with regard to our spreading generational separateness:

". . . In today's world children are deprived not only of parents but of adults in general. . . . What is needed is a change in our patterns of living that will bring adults and children back into each other's lives."

A rational scholar will not exclude data about the physical sciences which persist in breaking through with a statistical shout. Yet with regard to critical data about human nature, so many seem to be always "looking beyond the mark."

One would think it folly, for instance, if Holland spent a significant portion of its citizens' time and money destroying the dikes that hold back the sea; it would seem even more absurd if the Dutch people stood by cheering the wrecking crews! Yet, so much of what we are doing currently in our own culture is the equivalent of breaching the dikes, of removing tried and proven safeguards. So little honest attention is given to such matters as family and self-discipline on which so much else depends, yet others clearly pay a social price for the hollowness of someone else's childhood, and we all have a stake in each other's capacity for self-discipline! LaRochefoucauld's words seem to describe some of today's programs which are sincerely designed to compensate for fundamental family failures: "There goes another beautiful theory about to be murdered by a brutal gang of facts."

One of the "brutal gang of facts" of our time concerns the reality "of things as they are"—that citizens who are untutored in restraint and who are driven by their unchecked appetites can neither behave as free men, nor leave other men free; truth includes a knowledge of that harsh reality! He who is merely a "bundle of appetites" and has no capacity for self-discipline is neither educated nor free. A permissive climate is really a cruel climate, for it deludes its citizens into believing they must confront others —but not themselves; it elevates appetites by suggesting that we be accountable to these drives but not to people.

Real individual freedom is tied to truth, it is not freedom *a la carte*—not freedom apart from everything else— not just to the absence of restraint! Freedom is the catalyst in the chemistry of choice; it is not an outcome to be achieved by itself alone. Free agency in its fullest sense requires the individual to be in command of himself, for one who is a prisoner of his bad impulses cannot really choose; another truth about "things as they are," therefore, is that we either control our bad impulses or they control us.

We do not have much history about "things as they were" in the sensuous society that once was Sodom, but it is not likely that the citizens of Sodom decided at one gigantic civic rally to become the most wicked city in the world. The Sodomites simply sought pleasure, and things got out of control, and there followed lasciviousness, arrogance, idleness, and, significantly, a profound neglect of the poor and the needy. Indeed, sensuous souls often love their neighbors as themselves—i.e. not at all! Thus, Sodom was a free-wheeling, but very unfree society!

Education often gives little more than a curricular curtsy to those kingly truths about family and freedom, even though there is an alliance between moral absolutes and tactical ideals. It is a temporizing tutor who plays his bellows on the fires of student idealism, while insisting that there are, after all, no absolute truths to which idealism can be inseparably connected. Jesus did not drive the money changers from the temple because of vague or relative indignation; he was indignant his Father's house had been made "a house of merchandise!"

Moral education based on eternal truths is necessary for the development of the selflessness each of us needs in order to persist in serving our fellowmen, for relativism does not lend itself to an appreciation of one's fellowmen. It was G. K. Chesterton who wisely observed that, "The more we are certain what good is, the more we shall see good in everything."

Religion must, therefore, press for an emphasis on the application of truth and have a demonstrated concern for behavioral outcome. Rhetoric is an easy religion, and conversational Christianity makes few immediate demands of

us, while permitting us to exclaim and despair over distant
wrongs.

Our individually imperfect attempts at applying these
powerful truths are lamentable, but this is not an indict-
ment of the truths involved; man's early attempts at flight
produced many failures, but not because the laws of aerodynamics were unreliable.

Our perspective does affect our behavior and our view
of our fellowmen. In fact, when men and women look at life
through the lens of the gospel they will see not only more
clearly, but more broadly, the realities, obligations, and
opportunities around them, as the illustration suggests.

Life, or any particular situation, if viewed only through
the peephole of pessimism, presents a puzzling or discour-
aging picture indeed. Instead of wonder, awe, and pattern,
which the Christian sees, the disciples of despair disclaim
any knowledge of a "big picture" of life in which "all things
denote there is a God . . . yea, . . . and also all the planets
which move in their regular form do witness that there is a
Supreme Creator." The degree of divine disclosure—from
peephole to a picture window view of things—is up to us,
for so many today are like the Romans to whom Paul
preached and whom he described as follows:

"For the heart of this people is waxed gross and their ears are dull
of hearing, and their eyes have they closed; lest they should see with
their eyes, and hear with their ears, and understand with their heart,
and should be converted. . . ." (Acts 28:27.)

Without, for instance, some perspective about family,
an individual is apt to slip into social error or be confused
about the role of the state. Chesterton once wrote:

"Only men to whom the family is sacred will ever have a standard
or a status by which to criticize the State. They alone can appeal to
something more holy than the gods of the city."

Without a standard of truth, society courts subtle di-

saster, and the basic human hunger for truth goes unmet.
John Lukacs cautioned us about the need to balance our
concerns for truth and justice:

> "Our world has come to the edge of disaster precisely because
> of its preoccupation with justice, indeed, often at the expense of truth.
> It is arguable, reasonably arguable, that there is less injustice in this
> world than a century ago. Only a vile idiot would argue that there is
> less untruth. We are threatened not by the absence of justice, we are
> threatened by the fantastic prevalence of untruth. . . . Truth responds
> to a deeper human need than does justice. A man can live with injustice
> a long time, indeed, that is the human condition; but he cannot long
> live with untruth." (*The Passing of the Modern Age*, New York: Harper
> & Row.)

This is certainly not to say that we should leave off our
concerns about justice, but that we must begin to level with
ourselves in the context of truth. We not only need "the
truth" to avoid the random life, to see good in others, and to
meet a basic hunger—but also to provide a moral basis for
society. As Edward C. Banfield found in assessing the in-
capacity of citizens to cooperate in the area of Montegrano,
Italy, ". . . the moral basis of the society may usefully be
regarded as the strategic, or limiting, factor." Situations,
Banfield wrote, "may be understood, or altered, better from
this standpoint than from any other."

Without the anchor of eternal truths, men may
wrongly reason that the turbulence we have known in the
physical sciences is characteristic of all knowledge. A geo-
physicist said of the Apollo 17 moon trip, "Everything we've
learned from Apollo has been a surprise; there's not been
one correct guess." Scientists, or at least many of them, are
still open and capable of surprise and wonder. Perhaps this
is a vital clue for men in dealing with the "key of knowledge" to which Jesus referred. Rabbi Abraham Joshua
Heschel has observed:

> "There is only one way to wisdom: awe. Forfeit your sense of
> awe, let your conceit diminish your ability to revere, and the universe

becomes a marketplace for you. The loss of awe is the great block to insight."°

Sir Isaac Newton had this sense of awe:

"I do not know what I may appear to the world, but to myself I seem to have been only like a boy playing on the sea-shore, and diverting myself in now and then finding a smoother pebble or a prettier shell than ordinary, whilst the great ocean of truth lay all undiscovered before me." (Brewster's *Memoirs of Newton*, II, ch. 27.)

Thus the real "famine in the land" is the absence "of hearing the words of the Lord."

For the Christian, mental progress means hungering after truth and righteousness and growing as Chesterton wrote, "into more and more definite convictions. . . ." It is the skeptic who sinks "slowly backwards into . . . vagueness." Intellectual nomads and behavioral gypsies knock on many doors but turn away because the rule is, says C. S. Lewis:

"You must be asking which door is the true one; not which pleases you best by its paint and panelling. In plain language, the question should never be: 'Do I like that kind of service?' but 'Are these doctrines true: Is holiness here? Does my conscience move me towards this? Is my reluctance to knock at this door due to my pride, or my mere taste, or my personal dislike of this particular door-keeper?'"

So much turns, therefore, on one's view of truth and how deep his hunger is for what is contained in "the key of knowledge."

So far as its view of truth is concerned, the gospel is galactic whereas secularism is so insular! Little wonder the prophets have been so concerned with theological truancy —for it reduces human happiness.

Some individuals are simply too busy to be concerned with key truths; others mistake their particular secular passion for the purpose of life; still other individuals specialize

---

°As quoted by Edmund Fuller in *The Wall Street Journal*, February 2, 1973. Reprinted by permission.

in tiny tactical truths and shrink from the strategic truths of the gospel of Jesus Christ because the latter are not only difficult to accept, but "too large to be managed"; many souls are kept from the truth "because they know not where to find it."

The special, longitudinal truths of the gospel help us to feel more and to see more clearly our circumstance—a vital thing in this secular dispensation of despair. Each of us may begin like the young servant of Elisha who feared for the future until "the Lord opened the eyes of the young man" so that he could see what Elisha saw: celestial cavalry!

"And when the servant of the man of God was risen early, and and gone forth, behold, an host compassed the city both with horses and chariots. And his servant said unto him, Alas, my master! how shall we do?

"And he answered, Fear not: for they that be with us are more than they that be with them.

"And Elisha prayed, and said, Lord, I pray thee, open his eyes, that he may see. And the Lord opened the eyes of the young man; and he saw: and, behold, the mountain was full of horses and chariots of fire round about Elisha." (2 Kings 6:15-17.)

As the disciples of Christ seek to "stand in holy places" unmoved, theirs is a place with a view—a view of truth that, in a time of turbulence, can help us to "fear not, for they that be with us are more than they that be with them." For our own "holy place" can be a "heaven upon earth" when truth is honored as Francis Bacon prescribed:

"Certainly it is a heaven upon earth, to have a man's mind to move in charity, rest in providence, and turn upon the poles of truth." (Francis Bacon, *Essays,* 1, "Of Truth.")

2

A View of Morality

"... how then can I do this great wickedness, and sin against God?" (Genesis 39:9.)

"For as he thinketh in his heart, so is he. . . ." (Proverbs 23:7.)

"But I say unto you, That whosoever looketh on a woman to lust after her hath committed adultery with her already in his heart." (Matthew 5:28.)

"Morality, then, seems to be concerned with three things. Firstly, with fair play and harmony between individuals. Secondly, with what might be called tidying up or harmonizing the things inside each individual. Thirdly, with the general purpose of human life as a whole: what man was made for: what course the whole fleet ought to be on. . . ."° (C. S. Lewis, *Mere Christianity*, New York: The Macmillan Co., 1958.)

Where more truth and perspective are given, more is expected of men and women. In no situation is this enlarged expectation more demanding than in the realm of morality. Truly, the Christian knows that he is loved unconditionally by God, but also that, as the child of the loving and eternal Father, he is to be measured carefully. "I the Lord search

°Reprinted with permission of Macmillan Publishing Co., Inc., from *Mere Christianity* by C. S. Lewis. Copyright 1943, 1945, 1952 by Macmillan Publishing Co., Inc.

the heart, I try the reins, even to give every man according to his ways, and according to the fruit of his doings." (Jeremiah 17:10.)

Acknowledging a debt to C. S. Lewis for highlighting what I have since called three-dimensional morality (without wishing to make Lewis responsible for either that designation or what follows), here is an illustration which shows not how narrow Christian morality is, but how wide, how very wide it is.

Men are apt to steer a course in life according to what, how far, and how clearly they see, for surely, "Where there is no vision the people perish."

Lewis's penetrating analogy calls attention to all three dimensions of morality. The first kind is one in which an individual—

". . . is thinking it does not matter what his ship is like inside provided that he does not run into the next ship . . . the results of bad morality in that [first] sphere are so obvious and press on us every day; war and poverty and graft and lies and shoddy work. And also, as long as you stick to the first thing, there is very little disagreement about morality. . . . But though it is natural to begin with all that, if our thinking about morality stops there, we might just as well not have thought at all. Unless we go on to the second thing—the tidying up inside each human being —we are only deceiving ourselves.

"What is the good of telling the ships how to steer so as to avoid collisions if, in fact, they are such crazy old tubs that they cannot be steered at all? What is the good of drawing up, on paper, rules for social behaviour, if we know that, in fact, our greed, cowardice, ill temper, and self-conceit are going to prevent us from keeping them? . . . You cannot make men good by law: and without good men you cannot have a good society. That is why we must go on to think of the second thing: Of morality inside the individual.

"But I do not think we can stop there either. We are now getting to the point at which different beliefs about the universe lead to different behavior. . . . Remember that religion involves a series of statements about facts, which must be either true or false. If they are true, one set of conclusions will follow about the right sailing of the human fleet: if they are false, quite a different set. For example, let us go back to the man who says that a thing cannot be wrong unless it hurts some other human being. He quite understands that he must not damage the other ships in the convoy, but he honestly thinks that what he does to his own ship is simply his own business. But does it not make a great difference whether his ship is his own property or not? . . . If somebody else made me, for his own purposes, then I shall have a lot of duties which I should not have if I simply belonged to myself." (*Mere Christianity.*)

Concerning this third dimension of morality, George McDonald has said, "The one principle of hell is . . . 'I am my own'." Paul reminded us, ". . . know ye not that . . . ye are not your own?"

Just outside the strait and narrow course the Captain on the flagship has charted, and beckons us to follow, are reefs and shoals, and if we are to make safe passage, we need both a multi-dimensional view of morality and also revelation.

Without revelation the sea of life appears to be only chaos, but, once again, "the truth" when it overlays the human situation discloses not only purpose but the presence of a safe passage—not only the risks to be avoided but also

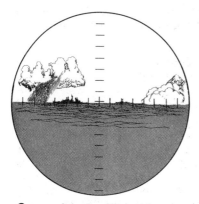

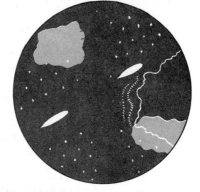

Seen with the natural eye   *Seen "with the eye of faith"*

the opportuities that lie in our path, the fellow seamen to be rescued and to be saved.

The wreckage and mistakes we see about us are there not because men are destined to fail in navigating the "strait and narrow" passage, for we come from a "Sea-going Family," as Thomas Carlyle perceived and expressed in a different way:

> "Man's unhappiness, as I construe, comes of his greatness; it is because there is an Infinite in him, which with all his cunning he cannot quite bury under the Finite.

Thus the morality that permeates a Christian's understanding is neither the Shavian morality ("An Englishman thinks he is moral when he is only uncomfortable"), nor the episodic sort of thing that breaks forth after a scandal (which Macaulay described as "periodical fits of morality"). The view of morality that emerges from the scriptures is one in which we should stop doing some of the specific things we now do, and in which we start doing some specific things we fail to do now.

In asking anyone, including ourselves, to accept the moral standards of the gospel of Jesus Christ, the Lord is not asking us to give up anything we now have *except* those

attitudes, habits, and patterns which will finally destroy
our body or soul! A man can keep his slippers but not his
pipe; a woman can serve in the community but must not
destroy her ultimate self-esteem as a wife or mother; an
individual can keep time for contemplation but must yield
on idleness; a man may keep his riches but must place them
second; an individual may go on loving but must stop lust-
ing; and men and women can seek out literature and the
arts, so long as they can give up or avoid sensuality.

There is not a soul on earth who will not be gentled,
enlarged, and refined by the influence of the gospel.
Whether we choose to respond to it, or to acknowledge it,
true morality presses in on us anyway.

"The truth is, we believe in decency so much—we feel the Rule
or Law pressing on us so—that we cannot bear to face the fact that
we are breaking it, and consequently we try to shift the responsibility.
For you notice that it is only for our bad behavior that we find all these
explanations. It is only our bad temper that we put down to being tired
or worried or hungry; we put our good temper down to ourselves.

"The Moral Law tells us the tune we have to play: our instincts
are merely the keys.

"You probably want to be safe much more than you want to help
the man who is drowning: but the Moral Law tells you to help him all
the same.

"Think once again of a piano. It has not got two kinds of notes on
it, the 'right' notes and the 'wrong' ones. Every single note is right
at one time and wrong at another.

"The most dangerous thing you can do is to take any one impulse
of your own nature and set it up as the thing you ought to follow at all
costs." (C. S. Lewis, *Mere Christianity*.)

Precisely because of the force of his conscience, the
Christian knows the adversary is "jamming" the signals from
conscience, hoping we will drift into "mainstream" and
away from the "strait and narrow" course. Satan also sends
out his own signals and seeks to put an unchaste society on

guard against prudery; to warn a relatively idle people about being overworked and exploited; to alert a permissive society concerning the dangers of authority precisely as that society is rushing headlong into anarchy; to prod alienated souls (who hunger for belonging and the sense of being useful and needed) to abandon the family and to avoid parenthood; to induce those wishing to be more "free" to build around themselves higher and higher walls of sensuality; and to tout "honest" books, movies, and dramas, but to avoid being honest with themselves.

In a society in which "anything goes," its members will learn too late that everything has gone!

Without moral truth men have difficulty measuring their societal as well as individual challenges and, therefore, in determining their response. Single-plane morality not only forgets the dead (and the lessons of the past), but it is also cruel to the unborn or the about-to-be-born:

"After all, children are not just transients in the world's boardinghouse, to be welcomed or turned away at the convenience of the older boarders. And if it is true that every newborn child should have a right to its share of food, it is also true that those who control the food supply should think twice before declaring that they no longer have enough for strangers and newcomers. In other words, the essence of the population problem—so far, at least—is not that mankind has propagated too many children but that it has failed to organize a world in which they can grow in peace and prosperity. Rich nations and poor alike have grossly misused the world's resources, both material and intellectual; neglected them, wasted them, and fought each other over how to share them. Thus the basic question is not how many people can share the earth, but whether they can devise the means of sharing it at all." (Otto Friedrich, "Population Explosion: Is Man Really Doomed?" *Time*, September 13, 1971. Reprinted by permission from *Time*, The Weekly Newsmagazine; Copyright Time Inc.)

Some, in their over-reaction to the rigid literalism of the pharisaic time, forget that the "Spirit giveth life" by showing how much more—not less—there is to be done in specific service to our fellowmen. A vague morality, therefore, is not morality at all, for it is as undemanding as the tame "Life Force" god with whom it is so often associated. As C. S. Lewis observed, real morality is specific and demanding:

> ". . . decent behaviour . . . means things like being content with thirty shillings when you might have got three pounds, doing school work honestly when it would be easy to cheat, leaving a girl alone when you would like to make love to her, staying in dangerous places when you could go somewhere safer, keeping promises you would rather not keep, and telling the truth even when it makes you look a fool."

True morality concerns mundane matters that secularism simply doesn't cover.

Thomas C. Schelling, in his important writings on "micromotives," used a powerful but simple illustration of our society's ultimate dependency on cooperation, selflessness, and sacrifice. Schelling notes how cars can line up for miles on a busy highway because a mattress has fallen onto the highway; in spite of the inconvenience to hundreds of waiting motorists, each driver, once he is safely past the mattress, does not stop to remove the mattress because, now that he is past that point, the act of removal would not benefit him. The capacity to act for the good of community similarly requires us to abstain from actions that hurt others, as well as inconveniencing ourselves in order to help future generations. As Schelling noted, "As in the cars that passed the mattress on a holiday weekend, it is hard to reach a bargain with the generations that follow." This latter capacity to anticipate, and thereby prevent, the anguish of our posterity requires the selflessness of a loving parent; it cannot be managed by those who are pleasure-seekers, for pleasure usually takes the form of "me" and "now," while joy is "us" and "always."

There is real doubt, therefore, as to whether or not, without moral education based on eternal truth, men can successfully manage their many and divergent micromotives for the benefit of the full community. Certain current trends are so separatistic that some individuals could become functional hermits—holed up like a missile—in the hardened silo of self-interest. Unless we really see each other as brothers, significant cooperation among men may not be frequent enough; mere biological brotherhood won't do it! In contrast, the Christian's filial feelings extend two ways into time, and "the hearts of the fathers" can be "turned to their children" in a meaningful mutuality.

Psychologist Allen Bergin has written perceptively about a view of life and morality in the gospel context:

> "The ideal of self-control is supreme. This life is a test—is a test—is a test. You have not passed until you have endured to the end and are dead. You will be tried every day of your life, whether you know it or not. Today, we are all bombarded by stimuli toward the loosening of moral controls. The provocation is enormous. You must practice self-control and have a strong repertoire of such abilities, so that when stress comes, you can cope. Mercifully, the Lord permits us small doses of evil to practice our controls on before we are hit with real temptation, but then it comes."°

Those who note the failures of believers in meeting some of life's tests are not facing the real issue. As Lewis observed:

> ". . . any man who becomes a Christian will be nicer than he was before. . . . Christian Miss Bates may have an unkinder tongue than unbelieving Dick Firkin. That, by itself, does not tell us whether Christianity works. The question is what Miss Bates' tongue would be like if she were not a Christian and what Dick's would be like if he became one." (*Mere Christianity*.)

A sage Chesterton said, "The Christian is only worse because it is his business to be better." True morality moves us into the role of witness and model, not because the Christian has status needs, but simply because lights have a way of being seen in the darkness.

Indeed, the Christian may even witness his morality by his silence in some situations. Theodore Roszak in writ-

---

°Allen Bergin, "Toward a Theory of Human Agency," Commissioner's Lecture Series (Provo, Utah: Brigham Young University Press, 1973).

ing of the "thwarted longings of men" recalled that George Fox chose to "stand still in the light," because Fox was "confident that only such a stillness possesses the eloquence to draw men away from lives we must believe they inwardly loathe."

Mormon once "refused to go up against mine enemies" and, as the Lord had commanded him—"I did stand as an idle witness." No doubt, as Roszak predicted of the wise man who knows when and how to do nothing, Mormon's voice was "like thunder."

Jesus' silence before his accusers in certain situations was "like thunder"—but only because he was certain not just about what was the right thing to do tactically, but also about what was right!

When the light of the gospel was bent by processing it through a pharisaic prism, it lost its fullness as Jesus so often noted during his ministry. When the light of the gospel was processed through the labyrinth of legalism, it was not only less illuminating, it was distorted. In the case of the Pharisees, scribes, and lawyers, the lessened illumination and the distortion in perspective resulted in a tragic inversion of values.

In the incident chronicled by Luke, the diminished light of the gospel was serious enough by itself, but when this diminution also combined with the failure of those who were supposed to be models (the Pharisees, scribes, lawyers) this cruel confluence resulted in both the models' and in other men's being hindered from entering the kingdom of heaven. When a model falters and enters not the gate, he not only ceases to play a positive role, and thus fails his followers, but he actually ends up also blocking the way of his followers— who might still make it, even without him, if they were not hindered by his personal obstruction. The faltering, or fallen, model has done just what Jesus decried: he has "shut up the kingdom of heaven." (Matthew 23:13.)

The failure of a model has many implications for his companions on the "strait and narrow way." Those who see the exemplar fail do not usually view his particular failure generously—as a reflection of understandable imperfection in an otherwise good individual; rather, the disappointed viewer is apt to see defective discipleship. Perhaps it is not fair that our shortcomings should be seen this way, but for the person whose faith is tentative and whose own discipleship is not fully established, gross or chronic failure in a "model" is often taken to mean that the exemplar is not, after all, really serious about his discipleship. Of course, we have had only one Perfect Model, but for those who are thrust—ready or not—into the exemplar role, it is important to remember that their lives need to reflect wholeness and congruency. In a life that is moving towards significant discipleship, the tactical lapses can be seen in just that context. But gross or chronic lapses raise the frightening prospect (for the onlooker) that the faltering is somehow strategic and not tactical.

One cannot help but wonder how many Sadie Thompsons there are who are nearly ready to commit to the straight and narrow path, but who have been deflected by a jarring experience. Sadie's bitter comment: "You men! You filthy, dirty pigs! . . . You're all the same . . ." reflected not only her disappointment in a supposed model, but her utter sense of emptiness in concluding that it is hopeless to expect to meet a good man. A person may be seen as struggling seriously to control his or her base instincts, or a person may be seen as yielding to his baser instincts, as if moral behavior is the anomaly—not badness.

We worry about sensory deprivation because of noise pollution, about nutritional deprivation because of poverty —and we are right to be so concerned. But emulatory deprivation—being without models and exemplars—may be the greatest deprivation of all. For exemplars not only show us that walking the straight and narrow way is possible, but that it is worth doing!

It is easier nowadays, for instance, with secularism's softened morality, for the adulterer to say that his impulse was simply unmanageable and that his behavior was so profoundly natural that he is not really accountable. Even more subtle is the rationalization of those who are immoral, but manage to create an aura of nobility around their acts, so that the sinner is the one who is terribly misunderstood and who is, therefore, somehow heroic. The trick apparently is to divert compassion from those who have been wronged to those who have wronged them.

It is only at the crucial decision points that one can tell how serious his own or another's commitment to morality is. In that sense, it is perhaps fair, after all, for onlookers to note our successes and failures at precisely those moral measuring points that do matter.

One of the reasons for our applying gospel principles is not only our need to validate truth, but (by experimenting with gospel principles in our lives as Alma urged) to achieve cumulative confirmation so that there is moral momentum in our lives.

It is, therefore, a fair question to ask of one who desires discipleship to what extent he can, using Alma's words, "give place" in his busy life for the serious application of gospel morality.

Part of the reason for the trend toward the religion of rhetoric, with its own rituals and dogma and one-dimensional morality, may be found in the changed response of some to the query "who is my neighbor?" In years past men's response probably reflected a narrowness of view which entirely excluded those not of immediate concern or geographic proximity. But our society today seems to have the reverse problem. Where once our circles of concern were too tightly drawn in terms of who our neighbors were, today our circles of concern are too large, too loose, and too filled with meaningless rhetorical regard for neighbors we know not and hence serve not, "neighbors" who are safe, because they make no real demands of us.

While the world is caught up with the smashing of forms in the arts and elsewhere (all in the name of freedom), what the gospel of Jesus Christ smashes are the conceptual and behavioral walls and compartments that keep men from being whole and congruent. The gospel presses us to align our public and private behaviors, for the gospel of Jesus Christ illuminates even the dark recesses of one's mind, where the battle for intrapersonal morality, too, is won or lost.

It takes courage to face up to the special perspectives that come with the fullness of the truths of the gospel of Jesus Christ, for one sees the human drama quite differently! Eternal perspective does not say to us to be inattentive to things like the dollar crises, floods, poverty, law and order, and borders—for these contemporary challenges represent, in fact, some of the interpersonal moral issues and challenges to our agency and to our ability to apply the gospel by assisting others. But in the fullness of the gospel there is also a warning about our being so caught up in the webbing and the throbbing of such events that we fail to see what other moral issues are at stake. We are clearly in one of those

". . . times when a whole generation is caught . . . between two ages, between two modes of life and thus loses the feeling for itself, for the self-evident, for all morals, for being safe and innocent." (Hermann Hesse, as quoted in *Trousered Apes*, New Rochelle, N. Y.: Arlington House, 1971.)

The Christian must speak out with the eloquence of example concerning the fullness of morality which is contained in "the fullness of the scriptures" in order to help others. While three-dimensional morality moves men toward Christ, secular morality has moved man toward agnosticism and atheism. Chesterton noted that "atheism is abnormality. . . . it is the reversal of a subconscious assumption in the soul."

Just as Joel Barlow could write in the early days of the

American Republic about how important "the habit of thinking" was to this nation's future (noting that if we believed enough in our equality as citizens, then our attitudes could spare us either anarchy or tyranny)—so our "habit of thinking" in matters of truth and morality can keep us joyful and free men—worthy sons and daughters of Him who gave us life and freedom in the first place. Without a belief in God—and in his moral laws—joy goes, too. Without the "why?", the gospel supplies answers to [concerning the need for righteous behavior], then, as Professor Earl Rovit warned, "Why not?" is "ceasing to be a question at all. It is becoming a kind of answer."

A View of Causality

"They seek not the Lord to establish his righteousness, but every man walketh in his own way, and after the image of his own God, whose image is in the likeness of the world. . . ." (D&C 1:16.)

". . . they have put no difference between the holy and profane, neither have they shewed difference between the holy and the unclean. . . ." (Ezekiel 22:26.)

"If joy itself be continually dampened by the thought of its own continuous annihilation, then only fleeting pleasures remain, unconnected in time. . . . When pleasures become disconnected, the intense ones stand out in prospect like branches stripped of leaves. They are thus sought directly; raw experience as such becomes the goal. Work becomes drudgery, nature becomes boring, humor falls flat, melodious music fades, children are nuisances (which they then become), sympathy and affection are perceived as "sticky," sexuality becomes unreal or dull, chastity is no longer worth the sacrifice, and freedom isn't worth a fight." (From the unpublished manuscript of Dick Hazelett.)

"When men cease to aspire to the ideal, the good, to self-restraint —whether in their arts or in their lives—they do not just stand still, but actually turn the other way, finding self-fulfillment in self-indulgence, and in an obsession with those three ultimate expressions of the totally self-centered life: sex, violence and insanity." (Christopher Booker, *Trousered Apes.*)

Different beliefs do make for different behaviors; what we think does affect our actions; concepts do have consequences. Therefore the attention given in preceding chapters to truth and morality. Secularism reverses the admonition of Jesus who urged men not to "omit the weightier matters of the law," for secularism—because of its distorted view of truth and its one-dimensional morality—inadvertantly ends up concentrating on the unweighty matters and leaves the weightier matters undone. As in Korea, unchaste servicemen in Vietnam have left orphans behind them—as many as 100,000 children in Vietnam. Funds are now being compassionately collected to aid these children who will find themselves stranded between two cultures and without a father. If we rely, however, only on contraceptives and cash—instead of conscience and chastity—we will always find ourselves dealing with harsh consequences instead of preventing misery. It is the dogmatism of secularism that blinds otherwise good people from seeing "the truth." One-dimensional morality will always fall short of what is desired, for it is our intrapersonal morality that shapes our interpersonal morality. John Lukacs has said:

"The profoundest problems of morality involve, after all, what people do (and how they think) with their own selves: in other words, what people do privately (or, rather, what they think of their own acts). It is therefore that the problem of sexual, that is, of carnal morality is at the center of the moral crisis of our times; it is not merely a marginal development."

Intrapersonal immorality depresses our self-esteem and the affected individual then becomes less sensitive and more disfunctional in the realm of interpersonal morality. The consequence of an incorrect view of truth and morality is symbolized by those fatherless Vietnamese children. The trade-off was typical of secularism—between minutes of pleasure for the sexual partners on the one hand, and on the other, days, weeks, months, years—a lifetime—of probable deprivation for their offspring!

Seriously adhered to, the creed of secularism can sometimes move men from heroin to methadone—but seldom to abstinence. If there is really no ultimate joy which reinforces proximate self-discipline, then proximate pleasure will win out. The only thing that varies is the method used to rob men of their joy and freedom—where once a Capone bootlegged alcohol, his successors now traffic in dope.

Secular concepts which are faulty drift, for instance, toward day care centers (not for the few for whom such may be truly necessary, but for all who wish to be "fulfilled," or simply rid of their children). As Sara Stein and Carter Smith wrote:

"Early learning in school can work in a limited way, but school will never be home. The complexity of family relationships cannot be reproduced. The bond between mother and child is qualitatively different from the bond between care giver and baby."

Thus in applying the teachings of Jesus—with their biting specificity—there are different consequences. One of the sins of secularism, therefore, is vagueness which reflects an uncaringness about consequences and about interpersonal relations. But another consequence of secularism is the vague, erratic, and cosmetic attempt to solve an immediate problem. Daniel P. Moynihan correctly describes the political behavior of Americans as "lurching from crisis to crisis with the attention span of a five-year-old."[*]

Verity in theology makes for accuracy in action, while doubt and disbelief lead to disjunctive action. Secularism has even drawn some churches behind it with the result noted by Samuel Callan, in which: ". . . the church will wed herself to the culture of the day and be a widow within each succeeding age. . . ."

Where men reject absolute truths and legitimate authority, there are subsequently no criteria for decisions, no direction, and no brakes, while an ever-present sense of hur-

[*]Copyright Newsweek Inc., July 10, 1972; reprinted by permission.

rying moves such individuals forward to "catch the fashion-able insanity." All too often we see a "perversion . . . become a convention."

Eternalism stands in sharp contrast to "instantism." "Instantism," writes President John R. Silber of Boston Uni-versty, means the "annihilation of cultural time through the development of an instant culture," and, finally, "the pollution of time," a form of pollution about which we worry too little.

Another major consequence of secularism is distortion in the diagnosis of human affairs. So often secularism blames "the system," making it the societal scapegoat, when it is the absence of individual goodness or self-discipline that is the real cause. Again, the view one holds of truth and mo-rality is pivotal; the absence of an absolute conceptual framework results in secularism's being "data rich and theory poor," a condition which adversely affects both diagnosis and action. Hazelett has said, "The secular world now knows nearly everything except why anyone should do anything in the first place."

We need both the humility and perspective necessary to see our situation and the governing realities that are "round-about" us as we are simultaneously "compassed about" and surrounded by secularism with its strange, mu-tant liberalism.

John Lukacs has said insightfully of today's deteriorat-ing New York City:

"Contrary to the liberal belief, the dissolution of authority and censorship has not lifted burdens off minds. No one can close his mind to the imagery of Forty-Second Street, no matter how he wishes to pass through it; a low kind of diabolical interest burns and scratches on the bottom of his brain, like a pebble at the bottom of a shoe. It is just as a bad smell clings to clothes. It is no longer in the material slums of large cities that the depths of modern degradation are to be found; it is in this slum of slums of the Western spirit. This most crowded of streets of the greatest city of the greatest country of the greatest civilization: this is now the hell-hole of the world."°

Since the scriptures, ancient and modern, speak of the time when *because* "iniquity shall bound, the love of many shall wax cold," can we really ignore iniquity, when it diminishes our capacity to love our fellowmen—in a world where the need for love exceeds the mortal supply? How we see each other and our situations determines how much we feel each other's elbows, how much we will excuse, endure, and expect from others.

Secularism may have helped to enlarge our perception of "who" our neighbors are, but now we need more help in giving more priority to needs that are nearest to us. There is something disabling about having too much of our attention drawn away from our immediate neighbors, for any abstraction of our affection lessens our active esteem of others and reduces our sense of accountability. There can be no development of ultimate love for mankind without much practice involving proximate people.

It was G. K. Chesterton who observed with regard to our microworlds of family and neighborhood:

"If we were tomorrow morning snowed up in the street in which we live, we should step suddenly into a much larger and much wilder world than we have ever known. . . . the typically modern person [seeks] to escape from the street in which he lives.

"But we have to love our neighbor because he is there. . . . He is the sample of humanity which is actually given us. Precisely because he may be anybody he is everybody."

It is what we learn not only in our classrooms, but in our family and in our neighborhood that is so causal and so telling, ultimately, in terms of outcome. Whether we enrich, or infect, our macro-world depends largely on our coping successfully with our microworld.

°John Lukacs, *The Passing of the Modern Age*, New York: Harper & Row, Inc.

Secularism tends toward hedonism, and as President Silber warned, "The popularity of hedonism lies in its minimal demands upon the individual." Secularism also tends to make an individual reluctant to "plow back" things of value into the society that has nurtured him: "One must not fail to provide his share of support for the conditions on which he depends," Silber reasons. As Dick Hazelett observed, some nonbelievers seem to be "parasitically drawing on the theism" of their ancestors while, at the same time, rejecting God.

Man can be so easily confused about causality! Bacon observed how "the fly sat upon the axle tree of the chariot wheel and said, 'What a dust do I raise.'"

Secularism's confusion about causal factors (and also its not owning up to consequences) can be seen nowhere better than in relation to the institution of the family and its declining state. Pitirim A. Sorokin wrote with wisdom and power when he said:

". . . it is much easier to grow in the family garden a large crop of creative altruists from newborn babies than it is to transform a grown-up egoist into an altruist or to graft an 'altruistic scion' onto a coarse, selfish stem. . . . So far, the method of 'family gardens' is the easiest and most fruitful way of transformation of the human universe from an ugly wilderness into a magnificent garden of Eden."

The gospel of Jesus Christ alone has provided the truth about the family. The Church of Jesus Christ of Latter-day Saints as an institution strives to resist the drift decried by many. Alexis de Tocqueville, when he visited America, gave us another reason to be concerned:

"Thus not only does democracy make every man forget his ancestors, but it hides his descendants and separates his contemporaries from him; it throws him back forever upon himself alone and threatens in the end to confine him entirely within the solitude of his own heart."

Gospel truths about life and the human condition stand in stark contrast to the world's view; the world's solutions so often lead mankind into conceptual cul-de-sacs. Without gospel truths, man's efforts to reach his goals are like the northbound explorer who drove his dog sled feverishly northward on an ice pack that was flowing southward— only to find himself farther from his destination at the end of a hard day's journey than he had been at dawn!

When secularism seeks to be a substitute for religion it is most dangerous, because it appeals to something inside man that makes for pretense such as occurred at the time of the Tower of Babel—but Babel has many modern equivalents. C. S. Lewis wrote well when he asserted:

"What Satan put into the heads of our remote ancestors was the idea that they could 'be like gods'—could set up on their own as if they had created themselves—be their own masters—invent some sort of happiness for themselves outside God, apart from God. And out of that hopeless attempt has come nearly all that we call human history— money, poverty, ambition, war, prostitution, classes, empires, slavery —the long terrible story of man trying to find something other than God which will make him happy. . . .

"That is the key to history. Terrific energy is expended—civilizations are built up—excellent institutions devised; but each time something goes wrong. Some fatal flaw always brings the selfish and cruel people to the top and it all slides back into misery and ruin. In fact, the machine conks. It seems to start up all right and runs a few yards, and then it breaks down. They are trying to run it on the wrong juice. That is what Satan has done to us humans."

What the secularists forget in reacting to hypocrisy among Christians (a real enough challenge), is that, as Silber said in another context, the absence of hypocrisy can mean "only that one has espoused no ideals."

But if, as Chesterton wrote, "Scepticism . . . removes the motive power"—secularism cannot rescue itself and it will lose itself "in quagmires of sensuality." Alexander Pope foresaw such a scene:

"Religion blushing veils her sacred fires,
And unawares morality expires.

> Nor public flame, nor private, dares to shine;
> Nor human spark is left nor glimpse divine!
> Lo! thy dread empire, Chaos! is restored;
> Light dies before thy uncreating word;
> Thy hand, great Anarch! lets the curtain fall
> And universal darkness buries all."
> (Alexander Pope, *The Dunciad, IV.*)

Leslie Fiedler sees "a weariness in the West . . . a weariness with humanism itself which underlines all the movements of our world, a weariness with the striving to be men." If nothingness is to triumph, why struggle?

Man's ennui and his frequent ingratitude for God's goodness to us is best described by Malachi: ". . . Behold, what a weariness is it! and ye have snuffed at it, saith the Lord of Hosts. . . ." Indeed, the interplay of despair, conflict, and commotion will mean that "men's hearts shall fail them," for the functional fatalist can rally neither himself nor his troops.

Great men can, and have, come out of economic poverty, but much less often out of an emotional ghetto. Thus while secularism sincerely seeks to tear down brick and mortar ghettos, it leaves the human debris of doctrinal deprivation in its wake and creates "a herd morality." For if there is no absolute truth, then, really, how serious is a tactical lie? Lest we think lying is merely a matter of manners, not morals, read what Aleksandr I. Solzhenitsyn has stated:

". . . violence does not have its own separate existence and is in fact incapable of having it: it is invariably interwoven with the lie. They have the closest of kinship, the most profound natural tie."°

As far as causality and consequences are concerned, the Christian knows that sins are symbiotic—that the "father of lies" wants his sins to move in squad, not in solitude.

Secularism rushes away from a belief in immortality

°As quoted in the *New York Times*, October 7, 1972.

which speaks to us of "was," "am," and "will be"—of "did," "do," and "will do," and toward "raw experience," to resignation, to boredom, and to futility.

As sons and daughters of God we can know "the dignity of causality"—if we do not hesitate to believe.

"For I should not rate highly either the wisdom or the courage of a fledgling bird, if, when the proper time had come, the little agnostic should hesitate long to take his leap from the nest on account of doubts about the theory of aerodynamics." (Charles Sanders Peirce.)

Part Two

Some Tactical Suggestions

"We live in deeds, not years;
In thoughts, not breaths;
In feelings, not in figures on a dial.
We should count time by heart-throbs."
—P. J. Bailey

Some Transitional Comments

As indicated in the Introduction, the style and focus of this book shift sharply between Parts I and II. In the war against evil, as in any other war, if the strategy is not sound, the tactics will matter little. Thus, the focus on fundamentals in the first three chapters.

King Benjamin, when he set forth the truths pertaining to the conditions of salvation, pressed oratorically as follows: ". . . and now, if ye believe all these things see that ye do them." (Mosiah 4:10.)

The same challenge persists for the disciple in each age: to conform his life to the requirements of the Realm of which he would be a citizen. Yet it is the unceasing requirements we each have to make, decisions bearing on the interplay of time and truth and minutes and morality—the tactical challenges—that seem to test us so. It is not just giving intellectual assent to the commandment, "Thou shalt love thy neighbor as thyself," but the specific, unrelenting, tactical challenge of how, then, to be truly effective in helping others.

What follow now, therefore, are a few specific observations about how the Christian can be a good soldier in his
tactical behavior in the midst of the fray. We must remember always, however, that hosts of others do good, desire
truth, etc. But these individuals are often cut off from the
wisdom of the Command Post; communications therefore
get garbled by secular sentries and mortal messengers. Of
such assaults on evil it might be said, as was said by Maré-
chel Bosquet of another sincere charge, "It is magnificent,
but it is not war." (Comment on the "Charge of the Light
Brigade.")

4

Some Thoughts on Managing Tasks and Time

Disciples of Christ must agree with H. D. Thoreau in his view of the relationship of time and eternity: "As if you could kill time without injuring eternity."

Spent time—like a spent bullet—tells us much about its "processor," for we see not only the residual slug, but indicators of how spent time is grooved by a man's soul, a reliable indicator of what a man is like.

No challenges of discipleship are more vexing than the management of one's time or the day-to-day choices we have to make—not always between bad and good things, but often between competing good things. These are precisely the areas where we need to apply our Father's morality, because these challenges are so real and so persistent. It is also at these confluences of time, choice, and tasks that we will achieve our greatest growth or experience the greatest failures.

Indeed, while there is a democracy about time as it is given to all men—day by day and hour by hour—what an unevenness emerges in how men use the time that is given to them! And time is, for all of us, a gift from God. Our first danger, then, in our attitude about time is the danger of thinking, as C. S. Lewis wrote, that each of us "owns" twenty-four new hours daily. That this may be our quantitative allotment is true, but it is given to us as a part of our mortal stewardship so that we can have experience in its expenditure and also that we may be measured, in part, by how we measure out our time.

A second danger in how we spend our time, and in how we approach our tasks, is that we will fail to see things in proper perspective and under-appreciate an opportunity or over-value a task. Once again, since tactics are derived from strategy, the gospel view of truth and morality must come into play.

There were no newspapers, as we know them, at the time of Jesus' ministry. Had there been, one can guess that the news coverage would have missed the significance of what was transpiring at, and after, Calvary, while perhaps reporting the return of Pilate to Caesarea after a trying weekend in Jerusalem, or while noting the arrival or departure of new trade caravans. The atonement, the central fact of human history, would have been ignored or subordinated to the other busy and important things of the time—unless the publisher had perspective about "things as they were."

Man's failure to develop a sense of proportion is not confined to the meridian of time, for it is with us today as one of the clear reminders of our mortality, not only on the grand scale just noted, but in little things, such as our inattention to our own children while we are busy feeling noble about some civic chore we are doing. Too many of us crowd out contemplation about ultimate things in order to brood about some real, but proximate, problems.

While the size of the four circles in the following illustration will shift in size somewhat depending on circumstances, the size-relationships of the circles representing "the things we ought to do," "the things we've got to do," "things we like doing," and the things we do for "other reasons" are fairly reliable indicators about our morality and also how clear-headed we are about the truth.

C. S. Lewis's observation which gave rise to this attempt to express the idea graphically is simply another interesting little test the Christian can use occasionally to check up on himself in his managing of his motives and his time. Obviously, a small "ought to do" circle and a big "like to do" circle suggest some room for improvement—unless one has reached the point when "duty has become a delight."

Our tasks are often without glamour. Duty, with all else that can be said in its favor, also has the tremendous tactical advantage of keeping us plodding along—even when enthusiasm and reason desert us. Some of the many extra steps involved in carrying another's burden a second mile may be taken because of love, but for those of us not yet so capacitated, duty moves many feet!

The challenge of managing time and tasks wisely tends

to have an outcome—either we use time wisely or it uses us; either we manage tasks effectively, or we are pushed about and prodded by them. The following observations about the interplay of time and tasks may be helpful, since there seems always to be more to be done than there is time.

1. Since our impact must be selective ("My life cannot implement in action the demands of all the people to whom my heart responds"—Anne Morrow Lindbergh), that reality requires us to do some goal-setting in terms of the outcomes we wish to achieve. Such goal-setting needn't be a hassling, hustling experience but rather a calm, periodic reasoned assessment of what we cherish enough to choose to do with our time. One exercise developed by Alan Lakein[*] involves the following way of highlighting goal-setting in the context of time:

A. Alone or in a group (such as a family home evening) write down in two minutes five major lifetime goals you have.

B. Next, write down in two minutes five major goals for the next year of your life.

C. Next, write down in two minutes five major goals you'd pursue *if* you knew you only had six months to live.

D. Finally, write down in two minutes specific ways in which you have spent time during the last week of your life that relate to the goals listed in A, B, and C.

This exercise in pondering (under pressure of time) tends to make explicit much that is often unarticulated. The exercise also tends to produce family-centered and gospel-centered goals—strategic things tend to emerge and mun-

[*]Now published in Alan Lakein, *How to Get Control of Your Time and Your Life* (New York: Peter H. Wyden, Inc., 1973). Appreciation is expressed to Mr. Lakein for permission to use his exercise.

dane tactical things to shrink in their psychological size. The last two minutes are usually the most uncomfortable for participants, because we see how unconnected our expenditures of time are to some of our real goals.

2.   High quality time spent at the "front end" of a task usually saves time later. So often five minutes of real concentration will yield more in the way of results than five hours of nagging but superficial worry. Unproductive worry —like Parkinson's proverbial law—tends to expand to fill the time available.

3.   It is sometimes difficult for us to accept the harsh realities about which situations we can influence as contrasted with those about which we can really do very little. The limitations of one's formal role, or geography, or his competency, etc., are vexingly real.

4. Of all the hours in one month, just one-half of any one of these hours can well be spent in anticipation of the demands that may come to us in terms of time and tasks. Just as the ability to delay gratification is a mark of maturity, so the capacity to anticipate is evidence of desirable sophistication. True, all the little "black clouds" do not become "thunderstorms," but often we are inundated needlessly; some individuals seem to be perpetually surprised, while others seem to be perpetually filled with Martha-like anxiety about the future. One can make a radar-like sweep of the horizon to identify time and task challenges while these are still manageable and while we still have a choice about how we will respond to the challenges.

5. The organizational adage, "the more parts, the more trouble," also applies to words. Multiplying words (written or verbal) may actually multiply the probability of being misunderstood; economies in expression (without being taciturn or aloof) not only save time, but usually are more honest and more clear.

6. Unless one assumes that the wheel of creativity turns perpetually and re-offers ideas and insights about people and things, writing down thoughts and ideas (and then "aging" these to see if the test of time can be passed) saves us rediscovering. Often we never recover what came to us once and went unused.

7. When one gets an unexpected gift of time as events and schedules get rearranged, a simple question to ask oneself is, "What is the wisest use I can make of this sliver of time?" To "deduct" several of the gift minutes in order to ask this question is seldom unproductive. Besides, it is good self-discipline to resist the tendency to simply "let go" and see what soaks up those unexpectedly "free" minutes. Since, in effect, we lease time to various tasks, when the lease is canceled, rather than watch the process of "subletting" occur without our, the owner's, consent, we should repossess those precious minutes.

8. Without making a fetish of goal setting, and without letting "lists" of tasks we desire to do dominate us, some recording of goals is wise not only for the self-reminder these constitute, but also for the satisfaction of "crossing things off." This, as with many of these suggestions, is a matter of style. Some can carry an agenda (complete with prickly reminders) in their head. Others of us need to commit rather explicitly to goals.

9. Some time needs to be preserved for self-renewal, for spouse, and for family. Few individuals have physical "retreats" (or activities), but most of us can at least build a small time shelter.

10. Decisions made in the midst of fatigue are seldom the best decisions, and agreements reached between the exhausted may last only until some of the participants are revived.

11. No equipoise is more difficult to achieve and to

maintain than avoiding an exterior style which tells others that we are too busy for them, on the one hand, and playing the omnipresent ombudsman, on the other. Good management of one's time can actually make more time available for people. But in kindness and in love, we have an obligation to help others avoid imposing on our time inefficiently or inappropriately. Except for real crises, if we have relationships of trust, we can without fear indicate that a particular moment is not best for us, offering a genuine alternative. There are examples of situations when even the Savior made others wait—for their own good. "Instant" help is not always the best help, if it creates in others the unrealistic expectation that such mortal help is always available to them.

Suggested by the writings of Anne Morrow Lindbergh*, the following illustrations call our attention to the disparity between what we care about and what we can influence. Moreover, as a friend suggested (when he saw the more common dilemma of the larger circle of concern and the smaller circle of influence), there are also situations in which individuals have far more influence than concern!

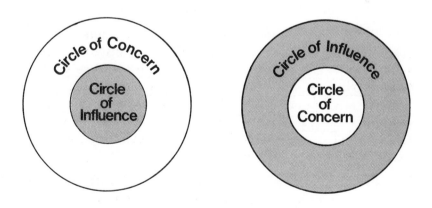

---

*In *Gift from the Sea*, New York: Signet Books, New American Library.

12. Since such a large portion of our waking hours is spent in one or another form of communication, some of our greatest "savings" in time can occur in these settings. Among the "shortcuts" which can be helpful, if carefully approached, are:

A. Asking the other person who is sorting out his alternatives what his recommendation is at that time, leaving him free to either describe and defend his viewpoint or back away from it. Getting "fact and feeling" out on the table can save time-consuming preliminaries.

B. Observing, to the other person, that while his recommendation is clear, his careful thought that produced the proposal must also have raised some concerns and, therefore, "What are the concerns he has or the defects in the proposal?" This can also give an indication of the objectivity and thoroughness with which the other person has approached the challenge.

C. Asking courteously, when needed, for clarification if it seems that the real problem is being circumvented with unnecessary delay.

13. Since we often generate either unmatched or unrealistic expectations about each other and situations, most relationships can be facilitated (and time saved as well as human pain), by our periodically taking time to report on how we are "spending" time and on how we are approaching a task. Audits of time need not be threateningly undertaken, but can be a mutually helpful—even an enjoyable exchange.

14. The quality of the time we spend with someone (or doing something) is almost always more important than the quantity of time involved. We all appreciate those who have saved money in order to do something special for us.

In the same way we sense, too, when someone has saved time in order to spend it on us, and we are glad.

15. As long as we follow Paul's counsel and practice "speaking the truth in love" and as long as all who are involved can manage the consequences, directness is usually facilitating. Directness—whether we are dealing with an organization or an individual—can often help us to locate and eliminate the "blockage" in communication.

The perpetual processing of the same temptation is both dangerous and time-wasting. Cycling and recycling the same temptation (instead of rejecting such blandishments out of hand) is not only to risk one's soul, again and again, but is to bring on fatigue, so that the Adversary may be able to do indirectly what we will not let him do directly. A lack of decisiveness in dealing with temptation (like David's fatal view from the terrace) ties up our thought processes and prevents us from doing good with the time alloted to us. It is a free man who can dispatch devilish entreaties summarily, the better to spend his time, talent, and energy "in a good cause." The same danger exists if we allow ourselves—after true repentance—to recycle our past mistakes broodingly.

There are two basic ways we can use time, for we will either use time in the spirit of stewardship or by being "acted upon." Chesterton said of Whistler that the latter "was one of those people who live up to their emotional incomes . . . hence he had no strength to spare." Some of us breathlessly "live up" to our income of time simply because we are being controlled rather than really governing ourselves and our schedules.

Man can learn self-discipline without becoming ascetic; he can be wise without waiting to be old; he can be influential without waiting for status. Man can sharpen his ability to distinguish (as the late Richard L. Evans wisely observed) between matters of principle and matters of preference, but only if we have a wise interplay between time and truth, between minutes and morality.

One of the more unique approaches to planning and to managing tasks has been refined by Professor Kent G. Stephens, now of the Brigham Young University. The ideas of Professor Stephens, and others who have pioneered a failure analysis approach (which started out as a way of avoiding failure in our United States Minuteman missile program), have become another tool for achieving success and are worthy of mention. Each of us can think of examples in human history when leaders have said, "That which I feared most has come upon me." While there can be no total immunity from irony in life, too often we drift unnecessarily toward, and fall into, the very errors we most fear.

We have also heard the lament of the failing parents ("Where did we go wrong?"). This concern could have earlier taken the form of, "How could we fail in rearing our children?"—with parents then planning, and acting, to avoid those undesired outcomes. In some respects, whether one is a dove or a hawk, America's recent involvement in Viet Nam drifted into a situation in which we experienced severe failures: we had an undecisive military outcome, while at the same time heavily draining from our national resources and the pool of patriotism. Some hard-headed analysis early in this challenge to foreign and military policy making could have set up some parameters and specific "monitoring" systems to avoid decision by drifting, an outcome that historians will go on trying to explain for decades.

Failure analysis is not intended as an automatic substitute for traditional planning but, on occasion, may be more helpful, and, at least, it can be a useful check on other traditional approaches to success, whether it is an individual or an organization that is involved.

Fault-tree analysis, a specific type of failure analysis, is so named because when the process is portrayed graphically on paper it resembles the branches of a tree. While the approach is too complex to be described herein, it is, nevertheless, based on some simple insights: identifying undesired events or outcomes, determining the probability of such failures, and stressing goal-oriented communication.

For those who are concerned with the effectiveness of approaches to some of our American domestic problems, Professor Stephens warns us that often our sincere social plans which are generously funded "appear highly successful in solving domestic problems, only to have disastrous secondary effects appear, sometimes 25 years later." It is certainly true that often the very way in which we try to solve one problem creates other problems which are at least as severe as the original one we are so sincerely trying to correct.

The point of drawing this particular approach to the attention of the readers is that God has done our "research" for us in this regard, and his commandments are the parameters for human performance. The failures to be avoided have been graphically portrayed to us and the specific behavior paths that could lead us into those failures have been clearly marked with warning signs. Indeed, the analogy given to us in the scriptures of the "strait and narrow path" is apt, for it is precisely the path we must tread. If we are drawn off in other directions or drift to either side, then we will become "entangled in sin" and we will fail!

By planning to avoid specific failures, highlighted in gospel admonitions, we can often move more directly, and with less risk, toward success. While Mormons may not subscribe to what has been called "Gumperson's Law" (the probability of a given event occurring is inversely proportional to its desirability), we do understand "that there must be opposition in all things"—for resistance and challenge are built into life itself. Also, laid alongside the much-to-be-desired consequences of gospel-living are the ways in which we could fail this mortal test, and the latter are described with at least as much specificity and detail as the positive outcome. The ways in which our entrance into the kingdom of heaven is blocked are also noted in various ways in the scriptures: "except a man be born again . . . ," "a rich man shall hardly enter into . . . ," "no unclean thing can enter . . . ," etc.

Since so often we share tasks as well as time, there are certain conditions that should obtain whenever planning or decision-making is to be shared. The ground rules are relatively easy to describe but exceedingly difficult for most of us to implement with any degree of consistency or sincerity whether as parents or leaders.

The usual blocks to a real sharing in decision-making include:

1. The needs of the formal leader to maintain his psychological size by keeping subordinates "in their place."

2. The genuine ambivalence on the part of the responsible leader about sharing decision-making in the first place.

3. The tendency, at times, on the part of the leader to think that the superficial exposure of his associates or the staff around him to a decision "in the making" is really sharing when, in fact, such sharing is simply therapy (or a plea for support) that occurs too late for the decision to be influenced.

4. The genuine (and often correct) reservations of the formal leader as to the ability of those around him to contribute significantly, or at least significantly enough to make it worth the extra time it may take to involve others.

5. The complexity and volume of decisions we are involved with can make the temptation almost irresistible to make one-man, arbitrary decisions rather than to "risk" opening things up to colleagues. Some decisions require

solitary action, of course, but as a constant pattern, solitary deciding can freeze out the staff and others from any real sharing.

The real values of sharing decision-making in proper circumstances include:

1. Getting additional and adequate information out on the table so that the decision-maker makes his decisions on the basis of more complete and realistic data, including "reading" the "feelings" of those around him about the policy under discussion. Feelings can be as important as facts, and can cancel out even the best plan as it is implemented against the "grain" of associates. A member of the staff could have some crucial data that could have impact on the decision at hand which openness can call forth.

2. Sharing can help the authority figure assess more accurately the consequences of his decision, because others may see implications he does not see.

3. Sharing can make it possible for subordinates and others to "invest" themselves in a decision or program so that their initial support and continuing commitment is more likely. "Investment" also tends to "guarantee" colleague or staff interest in, and support of, later necessary revisions as the plan or decision is refined.

4. Sharing tends to expose to the view of others not simply the "what" of the decision, but the "how," and the "why." Thus, they can interpret the decision more intelligently to those around them and give more effective support. Sharing also helps everyone involved to guard against developing unrealistic expectations about what will result from the decision. A "lonely" leader often generates unrealistic expectations about the changes his decision will produce, only to be surprised or disappointed later with the results.

Obviously, there can be real disadvantages to sharing

in decision-making. Generally, however, the disadvantages grow out of the lack of openness and candor between the leader and others. If the leader or parent communicates clearly and honestly ahead of time the degree of influence or involvement he wants others to have, they can usually adapt to almost any role—as long as they know whether the role is simply to be advisory, moderately participative, or influential and even decisive. If the formal leader implies that their role is to be decisive, but he is insincere in this indication, this will cause a reduction of trust that will make meaningful sharing more difficult to achieve in the future. Sharing can also cause a painful distortion in role perception by associates, if ground rules are not clearly established. Sharing cannot immunize the leader, either, from ultimate loneliness of making certain decisions or the responsibility for the decisions.

Size and functional compartmentalization obviously can mitigate against shared decision-making in the mundane, deadline-ridden world that leaders and administrators live in. Compartmentalization can also reinforce the stereotypes we have of each other. We are so quick to assume that a real contribution could not be made by someone (or group), because of our perception of their role, which may be a misperception.

Often, those who quest for a share in decision-making really do not want power, but merely proximity to the process. A wise leader can often provide this without risking his "sense of command."

The leader who is "not afraid" to make tough decisions and "crack heads together" is necessary. But, as the late C. S. Lewis reminded us, "It is so easy to break eggs without making omelets." An administrator can easily delude himself by thinking he is slashing through red tape and overturning bureaucratic impediments when, in fact, he is really cutting people up and removing barriers that were put in place for a wise purpose.

Whenever one is considering "sharing," "helping," and "time" he must also consider stewardship, and it seems, therefore, important to note that:

1. The stewardship principle *does not* mean "abandoning" those one is to lead.

2. The stewardship principle *does not* mean that some reports or performance measurements are not needed—but reports should not become the controlling element in the relationship of the individuals involved. (We must also be careful, in measuring, not to keep "pulling up the flowers to see how the roots are doing.")

3. The stewardship principle *does* require us to make clear to those we supervise what their tasks, roles, and duties and our expectations of them are, so that they can know what is expected of them.

4. The stewardship principle *does* place a premium on the leader's being a helping resource to the person who is being led or supervised. The leader should be seen as a friend and resource, rather than as a "threat" or someone who is always checking up.

5. The stewardship principle *does* involve accountability at all levels for the tasks assigned.

6. The stewardship principle *does* place a premium upon the leader providing not only orientation but also *ideas and inspiration,* which should be freely given and offered to assist others in completing their assigned duties.

7. The stewardship principle *does* lay great stress on the leadership style spoken of by the Prophet Joseph Smith with regard to *teaching correct principles* and then letting those who have so learned *govern themselves.*

At the heart of the stewardship principle is the need for us to realize that, while we can do much to influence others by persuasion, by example, by long-suffering, and by occasional reproof—in the last analysis, we cannot do the work of another person without eventually making it our own.

In summary, we cannot mismanage time, tasks, or people without misusing mortality; we cannot "kill time without injuring eternity." The words of Henry Vaughn are a fitting ending for these brief thoughts about time:

> "I saw Eternity the other night
> Like a great ring of pure and endless light,
> All calm, as it was bright,
> And round beneath it, Time in hours, days, years,
> Driv'n by the spheres
> Like a vast shadow moved; in which the world
> And all her train were hurled."

5

Some Thoughts on Helping and Communicating

"It requires tact and training to make it clear that because each of us can do so little in the great task of regenerating society, it is therefore more necessary that each of us should dedicate his powers and add his individual will to the undertaking." (Jane Addams, Introduction to Graham Taylor's *Religion in Social Action*.)

"If another person only had in his storehouse of deserved self-esteem what you had put there, what would he have to draw upon and to sustain him?" (Author.)

"Remember that to change your mind and follow him who sets you right is to be none the less free than you were before." (Marcus Aurelius Antoininus, *Meditations VIII*, 16.)

Probably no Christian act is attempted so often by so many with so many good intentions and yet with so few positive results as when we try to help others. While we sometimes have mixed motives for wanting to help, the problem in these situations is usually not motivational—it is normally conceptual and methodological. The challenges of giving effective help range from our frustrations in trying to respond to those who make it very difficult for others to help them—"How do you pat or spank a porcupine?"—on through to those circumstances in which individuals become like a sponge, soaking up all the help that is offered, becoming dangerously dependent on the source of help. There is a sad correlation, for instance, between youth who feel underwhelmed in terms of the things they are given to do in their youth and these same individuals who feel so overwhelmed later by the realities of life. In between, on the spectrum of circumstances, are hosts of helping situations that call not only for concern but for skill and courage.

Helping can be achieved inadvertently, and sometimes vicariously, and occasionally even where the helper does not really know the person being helped. But usually helping depends on knowing—just as does loving. While abstract affection can rise to the level of a generalized feeling, customized concern, real charity, and real help are facilitated by knowing what another person needs. Awareness makes it more likely that the helper can provide the kind of help in which real growth occurs in the person being helped.

One low-risk way of sharing things about ourselves (in an appropriate way) in a family home evening, or as colleagues in a working relationship, is the exercise, "My Individual Crest," which usually helps us to know others better and to increase our appreciation for each other. (See illustration, page 61.)

This exercise is quite simple. First, equip each participant with a pencil and sheet such as in the illustration (without the instructions noted in each numbered space). Second, indicate vocally what is to be drawn in each numbered area —proceeding one area at a time and allowing no more than one minute for completion of the drawing in each area. Third, after all six drawings are complete, then let each

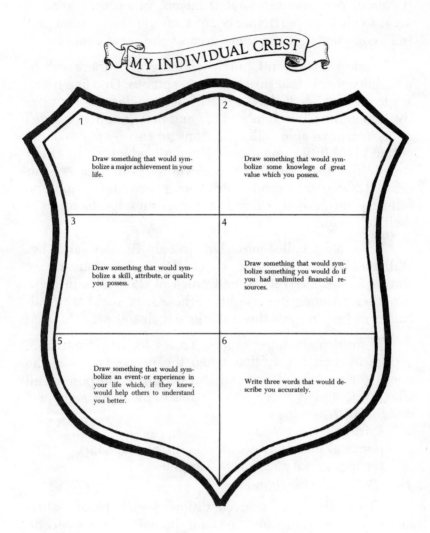

MY INDIVIDUAL CREST

1

Draw something that would symbolize a major achievement in your life.

2

Draw something that would symbolize some knowlege of great value which you possess.

3

Draw something that would symbolize a skill, attribute, or quality you possess.

4

Draw something that would symbolize something you would do if you had unlimited financial resources.

5

Draw something that would symbolize an event·or experience in your life which, if they knew, would help others to understand you better.

6

Write three words that would describe you accurately.

This exercise is the work of J. Ryck Luthi and Terry Jenkins with modifications by the author. Appreciation is expressed for permission to use it.

participant show his or her drawing for area #1, and say (in about one minute) what it means, proceeding area by area, so that all participants are focusing their "show and tell" comments on the same area at the same time.

Almost always in Church-related groups there will be a significant spiritual thrust in the responses. One fine friend made area #5 half dark and half light, signifying his reactivation in the Church in mid-life and that "mighty change" in his heart. An able colleague drew an ear in area #3, denoting his ability to be a good listener—which he is! Other friends and associates have in clever ways in area # 4 indicated a desire to send many young men and women on full-time missions to carry the gospel message to more of their fellowmen.

Two able colleagues, Dr. Joseph Bentley and Dr. William Dyer, of the University of Utah and Brigham Young University respectively, spend much of their lives in helping others. Among the insights of these men about the challenges of helping are those things which follow.

Definition: Helping others: To act (or to refrain from acting) in such a way that when the process is over, the person being helped has clarified his goals, purposes, and objectives, and is more able to reach them through personal growth in

    spirituality

    personal effectiveness (new skills or behavior)

    feelings of satisfaction or happiness

Two Different Conditions

There are two basic conditions which recur: when someone needs help and asks for it, and when someone needs help but does not ask.

Some Situations in Which One Needs Help

A person may find himself in many different situations in which receiving help from others is important:

1. He has a job or task to accomplish and doesn't have the necessary skill.

2. He has to decide between two alternatives and must make a decision.

3. He has more work to do than he has time. He needs another pair of hands.

4. He is experiencing conflict with another person and cannot seem to resolve it.

5. He is aware of a problem and feels angry, confused, or upset by it.

6. He is facing problems of such a nature that he feels inadequate and overwhelmed. His resources are not adequate.

Issues to Be Considered in the Giving of Help

1. What are one's motives for helping others? What are one's motives for asking for help? We need to understand our own motives as far as possible.

2. Sometimes people need to talk in order to feel better. Sometimes they need to act. In certain situations, listening to another is the best kind of help. In other situations, doing something may be far more effective.

3. We have different needs and ways of solving problems. Your way of helping may not fit with my way of needing help and we may not make connections.

4. When a person asks for help, that can lead to a dependency, which is often followed by resentment.

5. There are times when *not* giving help is the most help. People need to experience struggle and challenge in order to grow.

6. It is easy to give help for a short period of time. A long-range commitment is much more serious and trying.

7. Many times what people want is a friend. Giving

of oneself in friendship, unless natural and authentic, is a most difficult task. Many times giving of self to others is very difficult.

8.   It is easier to receive help, if one can also know the joy of helping too. Reciprocity in this dimension of human relationships is desirable, therefore, and care must be taken to provide such opportunities.

Question: What interferes with or blocks the giving and receiving of help?

Answer # 1.   If the prevailing atmosphere is one of fear and distrust. We can avoid ths block when the

Person Helping

Is able to create a climate of trust and concern by conveying personal standards of honesty and fairness and by expressing concern for the other.

Is able to sincerely offer help.

Person Being Helped

Is able to contribute to a climate of trust and concern by communicating clearly and honestly.

Is able to ask for help and recognize his need and accept it.

Answer #2.   If people are secretive or non-communicative and withhold important information. We can avoid this block when the

Person Helping

Shares himself openly; his feelings, reactions, opinions. He is careful, however, not to dominate the conversation, convey judgments or require that the other person feel the same way or have the same opinion.

Person Being Helped

Shares himself openly; his feelings, reactions, and opinions.

Answer #3.   If two people use or manipulate each other for their own needs or interests. We can avoid this block when the

Person Helping

Is careful not to use the other person in order to feel "useful." (When I'm helping others I'm important. Therefore I help others in order to feel important, disregarding the other person.)

Person Being Helped

Is careful not to use the other person as a place to "dump" or unload his problems in order to avoid accepting responsibility for his own actions.

Answer # 4. If a person is coerced, forced, convinced, or argued into one solution or another. We can avoid this block when the

Person Helping

Helps others explore many possibilities and alternatives; permits and encourages freedom and responsibility of choosing.

Person Being Helped

Seeks to identify and explore many solutions; accepts responsibility for choosing and deciding.

Answer # 5. If limits, standards, or expectations are not clear. We can avoid this block when the

Person Helping

Is careful to communicate standards, set limits and clarify expectations.

Person Being Helped

Seeks clarification of standards, limits, and expectations.

Answer #6. If superficial or hurried interactions occur. We can avoid this block when the

Person Helping

Takes time to listen and tries to understand the problem or issue from the point of view of the other person.

Expresses love, concern, and caring for the other as a child of God and a valuable human being.

Person Being Helped

Takes time to explain and share; presents the problem or issue from his point of view.

Expresses love, concern, and caring for the other.

In the foregoing, Dr. Bentley and Dr. Dyer offer much that is both practical and wise. Most of us can readily identify with experiences in our lives in which we have failed, or not been fully successful, because the way in which we sought to help ran us against one or more of the realities just described, as the illustration attempts to portray.

Awareness, communication, concern, and trust bring us together.

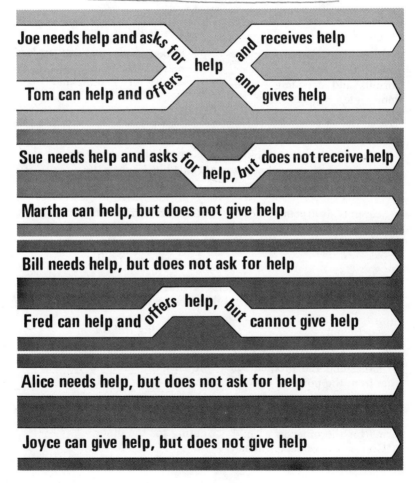

Joe needs help and asks *for* help *and* receives help

Tom can help and offers *for* help *and* gives help

Sue needs help and asks *for* help, *but* does not receive help

Martha can help, but does not give help

Bill needs help, but does not ask for help

Fred can help and offers help, *but* cannot give help

Alice needs help, but does not ask for help

Joyce can give help, but does not give help

Leaving out those situations in which individuals offer unneeded help, we are left with those situations in which individuals need help but are (1) too proud to ask for help lest this be seen as an admission of inadequacy, (2) not certain as to whom to ask for help or how to ask for help, and (3) not aware that they need help. Potential helpers are often in somewhat similar situations in that they could provide help but are (1) afraid or reluctant to offer help, (2) uncertain as to how to offer help, and (3) unaware that help is needed. In all of the above situations, the critical elements are awareness, communication, concern, and trust. Sometimes all we lack is simply an awareness that we need help or that we could help. Other times, we are very much aware but the level of trust between those involved is not high enough to permit the process of "asking" and "offering" to occur. Sometimes we are able to trust each other, but our communication is not complete or deep enough to sustain a helping transaction. The illustration represents four situations that each of us has, no doubt, experienced.

As is so often the case, the scriptures provide some excellent case studies, and this is especially so with regard to helping and serving others. We find, for instance the situation in which a direct, prompt, and spontaneous response to a call for help was exactly what was needed. In Acts 16:9 we read of a vision Paul had of a Macedonian man who said to Paul, "Come over into Macedonia and help us." Paul did just that and prayed and taught and baptized. The directness of the request was matched by the directness of the response.

We see in 2 Kings 5:1-14 a man of considerable influence and psychological size balking at the specific help that is offered to him by the prophet Elisha because the form of the help proffered was mundane and not dramatic enough to satisfy Naaman's status needs. Fortunately, Naaman's servants offered some specific help of their own by helping Naaman to see that the issue should not be the doing of "some great thing"—but to comply with the seemingly undramatic instructions of the Prophet. Naaman did as all of us who need help must do, at times; he accepted the reproof and feedback, and thence was helped!

While we cannot comprehend its implications, there was even a moment at Calvary when, as James E. Talmage observed,

". . . that the supreme sacrifice of the Son might be consummated in all its fulness, the Father seems to have withdrawn the support of His immediate Presence, leaving to the Savior of men the glory of complete victory over the forces of sin and death."

In Mark 9:14-29 a tender episode illustrates how vital it is for us to be able to be honest about the kind of help we need. The father of the stricken son is told by Jesus that help can be given his son, "If thou canst believe." Anxious for his son to be healed after years of anguish, the father cries out with tears, "Lord, I believe" and then adds honestly and quickly, "help thou my unbelief." Sometimes we can bring to situations "no more than a desire to believe," yet, even then, we can be helped!

President Harold B. Lee has said on occasion that three of the most difficult words for some of us to say are, "I need help."

There is also the need for us to take care in offering help, lest we appear to be condescending. Two-way trust in our human relationships can make it easier to ask for help. Trust can also reduce the chance that our proffers of help will be misunderstood. Of surpassing comfort is the fact that living righteously can give us the incomparable help of the Spirit in our communications with others so that the integrity of our intent can be transmitted clearly. Righteous living also earns us the help of the Spirit in knowing both what is needed and how best to help.

In addition to knowing about an individual in order to help him or her, we will often need others' help to help that individual. Our capacity to help will not always match the full configuration of others' needs—but by including the skills of others we can match and meet more of the needs of the individual whom we seek to serve.

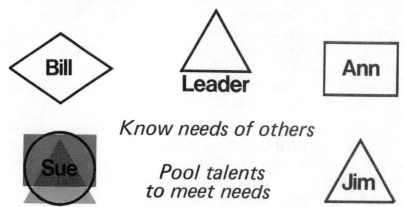

Jesus said the **king**dom is like a net "which gathereth of every kind" of person. Often rapport between certain souls seems instantaneous, and the "matching" seems almost automatic, as in the case in the illustration between the leader and Jim. Usually we need to pool our talents, however, to help someone like Sue, and Ann can contribute in this situation. The configurations of personality needs are infinite (to man). Indeed, as was observed in another context about a basic need, "It is not good that the man should be alone." While we may not be able to be helpful to others in every circumstance, most of us are under-used as helping resources.

A simple question we need to ask ourselves periodically is, "Whose needs am I trying to meet?" Some of our urges to help involve us in doing good mostly to feel good—not because some good needs to be done; the good feelings will follow the momentary "losing" of a small piece of one's life in helping another.

Neither can we, nor should we, expect reciprocity in

all situations, for the urge and capacity to give help often exceed the readiness of others to receive it. In sharing the vital truths of the gospel, we shall often find that, as Chesterton noted, an individual can be "already weary of hearing what he has never heard." So often the painful process of learning—including learning about spiritual things—must await the arousal of curiosity and even then Rousseau warns that we must not "be in too great a hurry to satisfy this curiosity. Put the problems before him and let him solve them himself."

In a masterful way, this approach was included in the way that the Lord helped the Brother of Jared (Ether 2:16-25 and 3:1-13) solve the problem of lighting the airtight vessels to be used in crossing the ocean. President Henry B. Eyring of Ricks College has artfully called attention to the way in which the Lord facilitated solving the problem— but without helping too much. The Lord helped the Brother of Jared to work out a solution. Later the Lord commended the Brother of Jared in one of the most remarkable experiences ever recorded.

Success in helping depends so much upon our skills in communicating. It is noteworthy that Paul's admonition about "speaking the truth in love" calls for the kind of glowing illumination that produces warmth as well as light in human relationships. The candlepower of candor can produce not only disclosure but *détente,* not only discovery but understanding. Usually in human affairs when we illuminate an issue it is not unlike using a flashlight, for we see better not only as to distance but also as to detail. Where we may have thought we saw shadows of resistance and malevolence in another, with illumination we see his fears and anxieties. And where we thought we saw only the silhouette of self-interest or sin, we now see a rationale. If we are loving and humble we can even see as Chesterton urged, "far enough into the hypocrite" to see "the virtues that he cannot" display.

An idea of C. S. Lewis once again lends itself to visual treatment.

What you think you are doing	What I think you are doing
What you think I am doing	What I think I am doing

Figure 1

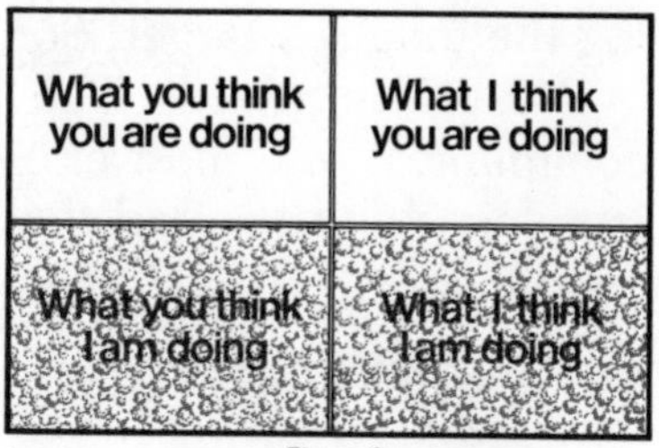

What you think you are doing	What I think you are doing
What you think I am doing	What I think I am doing

Figure 2

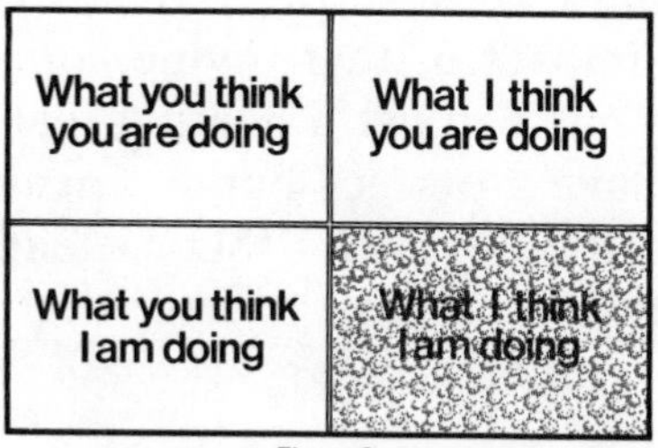

What you think you are doing	What I think you are doing
What you think I am doing	What I think I am doing

Figure 3

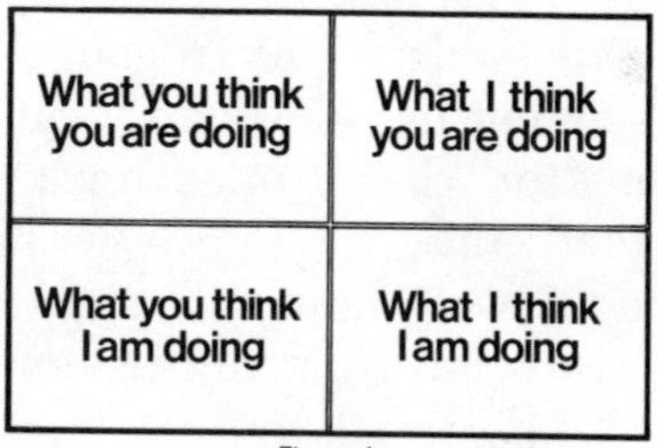

What you think you are doing	What I think you are doing
What you think I am doing	What I think I am doing

Figure 4

In our communication, we often need to check our perceptions with each other. So often we proceed apace, sincerely striving to communicate, but being seen by others as doing, or saying, something different than we believe ourselves to be doing. While some disclosures are inappropriate except in certain settings, the workaday world of human relationships can have many of its anxieties drained off and many of its relationships enriched, if we will but invest a little more time in communicating about our perceptions and expectations of each other. Surely no family home evening could be richer in sharing than those in life of this planet's first family, when Adam and Eve "made all things known unto their sons and daughters."

Among the less understood blocks to communicating are several worthy of brief mention here. Thomas Carlyle shared his discovery with us: "Sarcasm I now see to be, in

general, the language of the devil." In an age when verbal
karate has some sway, we must be willing to let the gentling
influence of the gospel tame the tongue—however tempt-
ing the tongue's target. So many of our soul scars are made
by words—not deeds. The senders of unhelpful and unkind
communications (most of us at times) use both some of their
irreplaceable time and their precious psychic resources for
"warmaking" instead of peacemaking.

In contrast, have you ever reflected on how the Master
must have felt as he heard his Father (at the time of bap-
tism and of Jesus' appearance to the Nephites) describe him
as ". . . my beloved Son, in whom I am well pleased"? It is
impossible for us to gauge the impact of that divine com-
pliment to a deserving Son, but one can get a fleeting feeling for what it might mean to have a perfect Father speak
that praise. While Jesus knew, intellectually, that he had
done well, how marvelous it must have been to hear those
words fall from the lips of the Father!

We are not wise enough to know when the need for
deserved commendation ceases, if it ever does. But it is significant that our Father commended his Son so openly!
Surely on our finite mortal scale of action we cannot dis-
pense with the giving of deserved commendation as a
regular part of our style of helping and communicating!

Geniality is a part of Christian communication but so
is accuracy. In the same way that vagueness in theology produces human misery, so vagueness in our communications
produces difficulty. Evan Hill in writing about the need for
accuracy said, "When we show that we care enough to be
accurate, a current of warmth is generated between people."° While candor often depends upon a commitment to

courage and truth, accuracy often depends upon our not
being lazy or indifferent about either issues or people. Fuz-
ziness in communication can mean that we simply do not

°In *Christian Herald*, June 1973, p. 24.

have the facts, but it can also mean that we simply do not care about the receiver of our communication.

More often, our patterns of communication show great unevenness in our capacities to receive and to send, as this illustration attempts to show.

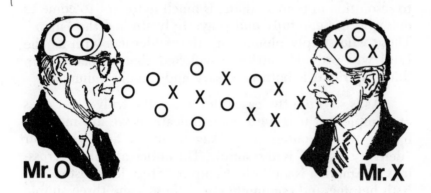

Mr. O   **Mr. X**

The imbalance varies with people and circumstance, of course. There are several things that account for the unevenness in our communication exchanges. First, each of us knows and feels more than he can tell. Second, some have more skill in sending than do the rest of us. Third, some simply have more to say and/or perhaps what they say is more relevant to the situation. Fourth, some prefer to practice economy in sending as a matter of style, so that there will always be fewer of their signals floating about to be received. Fifth, the filters and screens we have developed, individually, have different "meshes," depending on our experiences, values, and humility.

A major but subtle factor in communicating is, once again, our experience in having and utilizing the Spirit to help us. Some unwisely believe this divine aid is merely a convenience and a shortcut. In reality it is a skill of the highest order which has to be developed laboriously and painstakingly. While it is true that when aided by the Spirit, handbooks, manuals, and policies are, for that moment, not needed, it is equally true that personal familiarity with policy and mundane matters of administration is like having a "schoolmaster" who can bring us to a point of readiness for operational revelation in connection with our steward-ship. The special and sometimes surprising finding of a route to resolution in human affairs is much more apt to come to one who has carefully and prayerfully studied the "map." Those who simply plunge into the wilderness with a "the Lord will provide" attitude will find that scholarship in things spiritual is both necessary and usually unhurried.

As is so often the case with ideas (the truly great ones are simple), so it is with communication: we are most ef-fective when content is packaged simply and when our "delivery system" is also simple. The notice at railway cross-ings in America is a classic example: "Stop; look; listen." In both helping and communicating, these same three simple acts are also necessary.

One thing to be remembered is the harsh fact that no matter how much we improve our capacities to help others, (and we have a Christian obligation to do this), the mortal network of helpers is not always adequate to cover all con-tingencies—but even in such situations we are still not left alone:

> "When other helpers fail, and comforts flee,
> Help of the helpless, O abide with me!"
> (H. F. Lyte.)

6

Some Parting Thoughts

"Men's and nations' finest hours consist of those moments when extraordinary challenge is met by extraordinary response. Hence in those darkest hours, we must light our individual candles rather than vying with others to call attention to the enveloping darkness. Our indignation about injustice should lead to illumination, for if it does not, we are only adding to the despair—and the moment of gravest danger is when there is so little light that darkness seems normal!" (Author.)

A recent physical ailment of shoulder and arm (which a doctor and therapist helped to explain) assisted me in appreciating the interconnectedness of tendons, muscles, and nerves. Some of the pain was not primary pain but was referred pain; discomfort at one point had no visible connection with pain elsewhere—and yet it did. No dramatic single applied treatment could be made at one point that would ease the pain: several things had to be done together with patience. So it often is with life's challenges and spiritual matters: there is far more interconnectedness than we like to admit between beliefs and behavior, between concepts and conduct, between causality and consequences.

Pain in society that expresses itself in an arm of government may be referred pain from inflamed homes; numbness in values may disappear only when truth is more widely circulated; spasms in moral muscles will cease only when we approach morality with an appreciation for its multi-dimensional nature.

This book has briefly discussed fundamental, strategic things like truth and morality. For if an individual has no strategic fortress to defend, tactics do not matter much. If an individual does not see those about him as his brothers and sisters in perpetuity, then rather than saying, ". . . what is past my help is past my care," he may well indicate that those beyond his caring are beyond his helping, too.

A disciple will understand, too, that it is just as wrong to hurt himself as it is to hurt others, because we are so interdependent, for just as what we do to others affects self, so what we do to self affects others. Lewis gives us a useful clue that lies so close to most of us that we miss it:

"For a long time I used to think this a silly, straw-splitting distinction: how could you hate what a man did and not hate the man? But years later it occured to me that there was one man to whom I had been doing this all my life—namely myself. However much I might dislike my own cowardice or conceit or greed, I went on loving myself. There had never been the slightest difficulty about it. In fact the very reason why I hated the things was that I loved the man."

We do not have to accept sin in self or others in order to love. If we are willing to strive for righteousness that is based on truth and morality, we will find greater happiness as we manage better our time and tasks and the process of helping others.

To be sure, travail in some form is the lot of Christians as well as other mortals. If we can but believe with Paul that in the economy of God our challenges will not be "above that ye are able . . . to bear," and have faith in who we are, then, perhaps, the words of Marcus. Aurelius Antoninus and of Nephi will speak to us:

"Nothing happens to any man that he is not formed by nature to bear." (*Meditations II.*)

"I will go and do the things which the Lord hath commanded, for I know that the Lord giveth no commandments unto the children of men, save he shall prepare a way for them that they may accomplish the thing which he commandeth them." (1 Nephi 3:7.)

Let the benediction of this book include the simple but eloquent language (to which Elder Gordon B. Hinckley has fortunately called our attention) of a pioneer girl who experienced tactical tragedy because of her belief in the strategic truth. Concerning the Mormon migration to western America in the mid-nineteenth century, she recalled:

"We traveled from fifteen to twenty-five miles a day . . . till we got to the Platte River. . . . We caught up with the handcart companies that day. We watched them cross the river. There were great lumps of ice floating down the river. It was bitter cold. The next morning there were fourteen dead. . . . We went back to camp and had our prayers and . . . sang "Come, Come, Ye Saints, No Toil Nor Labor Fear." I wondered what made my mother cry that night. . . . The next morning my little sister was born. It was the twenty-third of September. We named her Edith. She lived six weeks and died. . . . She was buried at the last crossing of the Sweetwater.

"When we arrived at Devils Gate, it was bitter cold. We left many of our things there. . . . My brother, James . . . was as well as he ever was when we want to bed that night. In the morning he was dead. . . .

"My feet were frozen; also my brother's and my sister's. It was nothing but snow. We could not drive the pegs in our tents. . . . We did not know what would become of us. Then one night a man came to our camp and told us . . . Brigham Young had sent men and teams to help us. . . . We sang songs; some danced, and some cried. . .

"My mother had never got well. . . . She died between the Little and Big Mountains. . . . She was 43 years of age. . . .

"We arrived in Salt Lake City nine o'clock at night the eleventh of December, 1856. Three out of the four that were living were frozen. My mother was dead in the wagon. . . .

"Early next morning Brigham Young came. . . . When he saw our condition, our feet frozen and our mother dead, tears rolled down his cheeks. . . .

"The doctor amputated my toes . . . while the sisters were dressing mother for her grave. . . . When my feet were fixed they carried us in to see our mother for the last time. . . . That afternoon she was buried. . . .

"I have thought often of my mother's words before we left England. 'Polly, I want to go to Zion while my children are small so they can be raised in the Gospel of Jesus Christ, for I know this is the true church.'" (*Autobiography of Mary Goble Pay*, Church Archives, The Church of Jesus Christ of Latter-day Saints.)

While it is no longer necessary in the same sense to find a geographic Zion, the same uncomplaining dedication will be required of those who pursue discipleship. And in the midst of the dedication of those like the woman who recorded this poignant episode, or in the commitment of Paul, who could say, after his own ordeals, "I have fought a good fight, I have finished my course, I have kept the faith," there will often be some disparity between the disciple's capacity for appreciation and his powers of articulation.

One simply cannot come to a cause like the kingdom of God, with its celestial concepts, and not appreciate and identify with what Ammon said: "Behold, I say unto you, I cannot say the smallest part which I feel."

INDEX